# An Anthology of Poetry for Shakespeare

# An Anthology of Poetry for Shakespeare

*Selected by Charles Osborne*
*Illustrated by Louis le Brocquy*

Bishopsgate Press
Southwark 1988

The cover and illustrations within by LOUIS le BROCQUY are studies towards an image of WILLIAM SHAKESPEARE and are reproduced by kind permission of the artist.

**British Library Cataloguing in Publication Data**

Anthology of poetry for Shakespeare

1. Poetry in English. Special subjects. Drama in English Shakespeare, William, 1564 - 1616. Anthologies

I. Osborne, Charles, 1927 -
821'.008'0351

ISBN 185219 021 3

All enquiries and requests relevant to this title should be sent to the publisher, Bishopsgate Press Ltd., 37, Union Street, London, SE1 1SE

Printed by Whitstable Litho Printers Ltd., Whitstable, Kent.

# FOREWORD

This collection celebrates a happy moment in the posthumous life of Shakespeare. Over the last fifteen years or so, one interesting drama on the fringe of the world of Drama has been the spectacle of Sam Wanamaker battling to realise the dream of rebuilding Shakespeare's Globe theatre on its original site. From time to time, the air carried rumours of his imminent defeat. But each year he re-emerged undaunted. And in most of these years he invited a wide variety of poets to contribute poems about or in some way connected with Shakespeare for a published collection to celebrate his continuing campaign. His persistence gained its reward. In 1987, against all obstacles, he won the first but crucial victory and secured that vital plot of ground on which the theatre can now be built.

To mark this victory, a selection from the poems in the ten celebratory collections published so far has been made by Charles Osborne.

Sam Wanamaker's Globe enterprise has always found ready support from poets. One wonders what playwrights make of it. Merely to ask the question produces a fairly clear reply. Modern British playwrights display in their work little filial regard for Shakespeare. Not surprising, considering how, for some three centuries, like Saturn he devoured nearly all his dramatic inheritors alive. Towards poets, on the other hand, he seems to have proved less of a cannibal father, more of a nurturing mother. At least, that's how it has appeared to the poets. Pasternak divined this, during his years of translation, when he realised that the intriguing family likeness, the peculiar 'charm', that all British poets seemed to share, was nothing other than the presence, somehow behind and within all of them, of Shakespeare.

He was speaking of the British poets of the 19th Century and earlier. Whether more recent British poets have been quite so susceptible to this particular parental fixation is a nice question. It's not easy to imagine how they could escape entirely. Shakespeare's presence in the land does not lessen. His prestige as a poet, as the very genius of the language, does not fall.

And sure enough, quite a few of the poems in this collection reveal poets who are, at bottom, preoccupied by Shakespeare, unconsciously or not, in the old-fashioned way. Probably, among British poets in general, that has not changed much. What certainly has changed is the available range of means by which poets can distance themselves from a preoccupation of that sort; and the apparent absence of Shakespeare's influence, of his 'charm', from the verbal manners of some of these poems, need mean no more than that the Shakespearean inheritance has submerged, or has been deliberately stowed away, out of sight. Where this has happened, the sacred relics then radiate not so much from the substance of the verse as from something in the basic attitude of the poet, something like a conscience---a background dependance on a certain sense of humanity, a particular system of values. This shows through in the most unlikely places. It is exactly this which makes the jauntily up-to-date and very funny pieces by D.J. Enright and Edwin Morgan finally so moving and memorable. In this sense, such poems do carry the 'charm' and belong to the lineage that Pasternak would have recognised.

The pieces here by poets of other nationalities, free of the familial root in the Shakespearean bequest, provide glimpses of what can happen when his genes migrate. The most significant sign, though, of what is going on in Shakespeare's empire, is perhaps the fact that this very

English dream---the dream of raising the Globe out of its ashes---is now to be realised by an American. Maybe Sam Wanamaker would prefer to call it an American or better still a Universal dream. Whoever claims the dream, we islanders can be grateful to him, and the outcome should please everybody.

**TED HUGHES**

**TED HUGHES**

**A FULL HOUSE**

**1. Queen Of Hearts**

Venereal, uterine heat.
Smothering breast-fruit.
The poor boy gasped to be out.

Hell-mouth he could hear.
The many mouthed hound in there
Started his heart a hare.

Daddy jumped, the god of war,
From under her skirts, as a scythe-tusked boar.
Mortal frailty tore.

Willy's blood a shower
Of fertiliser for,
Where he fell, a flower.

## 2. Queen of Spades

The Serpent Of Old Nile
Coilded in a fig-tree
Queen Cleopatra's
Affable, familiar
Hypodermic smile.

Fruit of the tree he seized
And was darkly kissed.
And melted into air
Twenty years had gone
Dreaming of passion on
That bed in the East.

### 3. Queen of Clubs

Three Corbies in a tree
Sang to Macbeth
Maid, Wife, Mother
We are tragedy
Queen of Birth and Death
And there is no other.

Your Fate's a double coil.
For Will to grab the crown
Mother, Maid, Wife
You must kill your Soul
(We'll help you get it done)
And still hang on to your life.

Such soulful, wilful acts
The shadows of your limbs
Wife, Mother, Maid
Shall be history's facts...
The crown grabbed in these dreams
Paid for by Cromwell's head.

### 4. Queen of Diamonds

My son told such a tale...
His father killed by an Owl!

Dressed for the funeral
He started to play the Fool.

Dreaming he'd married me
He cried: 'It cannot be!'

His sanity took the veil
In Avon's darkest pool.

Succession in a pall
Crazed him to murder us all...

Pausing for no farewell
I fled into this pearl.

## 5. King of Hearts

My Will shall be
What I have planned:
My treasure, my land
Split into three.

One third I pay
To help Anne's age
Put her youth's rage
And hate away.

To Judith one
For who will marry
Memento Mori
Of my son?

And for Sue
The final part
Includes my heart
That is pierced through

By my own Lance
In young Edmund's
Bastard Edmund's
Lineal hands.

Envoi

And to God, Her
    Of triple power
Locked with the hoodlum
    Of this hour.

### 6. King of Spades

Tarquin the King's
Besieging eye
Sacked Lucrece's
Chastity.

Which, it seems,
Wore such a crown
Kingship itself
Was tumbled down.

The bubble of State
We see from this
Balloons from lips
That were made to kiss.

## 7. King of Clubs

A cripple soon
Can smell a fault.
Speak of my lameness
I straight will halt.

I carry a sack
Of limbless pain.
Body deposed
The mind will reign.

The nimble fools
Of human pride
Shall be the toys
Of what I hide.

## 8. King of Diamonds

The Cabalist is old.
Crucibles thrice thirteen
Alchemised air to gold,

His soul's incarnate stain,
The tigerish, upstart crow,
To a self of diamond stone.

Sword and Cup can go;
All trumpery that held
The invisible in awe.

Familiar, daemon child,
A howling banshee, rides
A rainbow from the world.

And as the pageant fades,
Warming his master's grave
The calloused Golem hides

Clutching the broken staff
Three fathoms under the prayer
And terminal, wild laugh

Of his great lord who prays
The sea-monster ashore
And feeds it with his plays.

### 9. Knave of Hearts

Hal moistens his lips.
  After many a try
At last he slips
  Through the needle's eye

To sew the tap-
  -estry of a new England.
But he's only the tip
  Of the glory-hole tangle

Old Adam packed in
  To the quaking sack
Of the fat Knight's skin...
  Will the thread break?

### 10. Knave of Spades

The Sulphur, Charcoal, Nitrate of his gunnery
Proportioned Othello.
Who fell for this fellow?
A blonde pure as a taper in a nunnery.

A light, light lass, a dark, heavy chap,
And a touch of evil laughter...
Boom, the whole lot goes up
Unhappily ever after.

## 11. Knave of Clubs

Nature's child
Looks at men' graves
As the sun
Watches the waves.

And as the wind
Does what it likes
Finds no bar
To his thoughts and looks.

Wherefore should he
Be other than
Death itself
To play at man?

For all it needs
To rule alone
Taking all
Is to love none.

## 12. Knave of Diamonds

As Mary bore
The Son so mourned
Tortured, murdered
And returned

Timon gives all.
Hands close and take.
Open to render
Hatred back.

In X-ray blink
Baboons revealed
The skulls for which
Their lips had smiled.

He hurls the bomb
From his mother's womb
That blows the species
To kingdom come.

### 13. Joker

On all my stages
Not to be heard
On all my pages
Never a word

Where there is nobody
A soothing
Suffering all
Suffers nothing

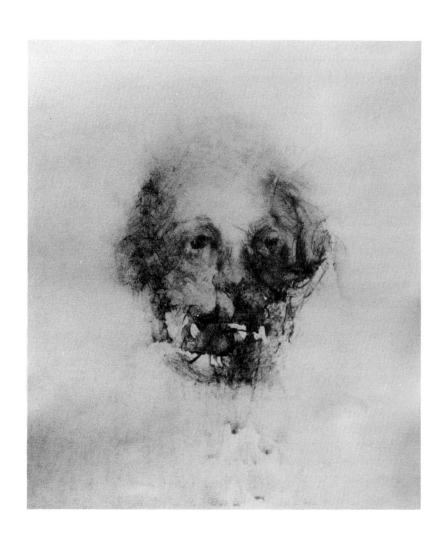

## C. DAY LEWIS

## HYMN FOR SHAKESPEARE'S BIRTHDAY

The Word was the beginning,
Spirit's and Reason's sire —
Sent the chartered planets spinning
Down their tracks of fire.
After that fiery birth
What endless aeons throng
Before this green and troubled earth
Can grow to her full song!

The all-creative Word
Surveying earth's huge span
From every maker there preferred
One man to speak for Man —
Gifted with art beyond
The best who'd worn the bays,
Sure pilot still on the profound
Heart's uncharted ways.

This man, whose vision ranged
Life's whole from bliss to woe,
Perceived how love, warped or estranged,
Will bring the highest low.
Today his birthday fell.
But he is born once more
Each time we come beneath his spell
And to his genius soar.

# W.H. AUDEN

## TALKING TO MICE

Plural the verdicts we cast on the creatures we have
    to shake hands with:
*Creepy! Get HER! Good Lord, what an oddity! One
    to steer clear of!*
*Fun! Impossible! Nice, but a bore! An adorable
    monster!*
But those animates which we call in our arrogance
    *dumb* are
judged as a species and classed by the melodramatic
    division,
either *Goodies* or *Baddies.* So spiders and roaches
    and flies we
excommunicate as - ugh!— all irredeemably evil,
*Dreck* to be stamped on or swatted, abolished without
    any hover.
Mice, *per contra*, except to a few hysterical women,
rank among the most comely of all the minature
    mammales
who impinge on our lives, for smell doesn't
    seem to alarm them,
visitors whom we can jump with, co-agents it doesn't
    seem phoney
we should endow with a *You,*as from now on I shall in
    these verses,
though my grammatical shift will be out of your ken
    for, alas, you
never have managed, all successful parasites
    must, to
crack the code of your host, wise up on what habits
    can travel.
Ah!, if only you had, with what patience would
    have trained you
how to obtemper your greeds, recalling the way that
    our Nannies
moulded our nusery *moeurs*, bechiding whenever we
    turned our

noses up at a dish - *Now remember the starving
  Armenians! -*
and when we gobbled - *Enough! Leave something for
  nice Mr. Manners! -*
cited you suitable maxims. *Good Little Mice never
  gnaw through*
*wood work or nibble at packages.  Good Little Mice
  never scatter*
*droppings that have to be swept up.  Good Little Mice
  get a tid-bit,*
*Bad Little Mice die young.* Then, adapting an adage
  of lovers,
*Two Little Mice are a company, Three Little Mice
  are a rabble.*


All through the Spring and the Summer, while you
  were still only a couple,
fit-sides we dwelt in a peace as idyllic as only a
  Beatrix
Potter could paint.  In September, though, this was
  abrupted: you must have
littered for, lo!, quite suddenly, there were a swarm
  of you, messing
everything up until no cache was aloof to your insults.
What occurred now confirmed that ancient political
  axiom:
*when Words fail to persuade, then Physical Force
  gives the orders.*
Knowing you trusted in us and would never believe
  an unusual
object pertaining to men could be there for a sinister
  purpose,
traps were baited and one by one you were fatally
  humbugged.


All fourteen of you perished. To move from where
  we'd been sipping
cocktails and giving ear, translated out of ourselves,
  to
Biedermeyer Duets or Strauss in *Metamorphosen,*

24

mourning the end of his world, and enter the kitchen
  to find there
one more broken cadaver, its black eyes beadily
  staring,
obumbrated a week. We had felt no talent to murder,
it was against our pluck. Why, why then.  For
  *raisons d'Etat.* As
householders we had behaved exactly as every State
  does,
when there is something it wants, and a minor one
  gets in the way.

## STEPHEN SPENDER

## LATE STRAVINSKY LISTENING
## TO LATE BEETHOVEN

'At the end, he listened only to
Beethoven's Posthumous Quartets.
Some we played so often
You only heard the needle in the groove.

(She said; and smiled through her locked tears,
Lightly touching her cheek.)

    Yes, lying on your bed under the ceiling,
Weightless as a feather, you became
Free of every self but the transparent
Intelligence through which the music showed
Its furious machine.  Delectable to you
Beethoven's harsh growlings, hammerings,
Crashings on plucked strings, his mockery at
The noises in his head, imprisoning him
In shouting deafness.
                What was sound outside
His socketed skull, he only knew
Through seeing things make sounds.  For example,
Walking through the field one clear March day
He saw a shepherd playing on his pipe
And knew there was the tune because he saw it
Jigging white against the green
Hillside.  Then stumping down into the valley
Saw colliding blocks of thawing floes
Clash cymbals unheard between banks,
Saw too the wind high up pluck the dumb strings
Of willow harps.
            Music became
The eye-hole of his skull through which he looked
Beyond the barred and shutting discords on
A landscape all of sound.  It drew above

26

A base of mountain crags, a bird, a violin,
In a vast sky, its flight the line
A diamond cuts on glass, parabola
Held in the hearing eye.  Flew on flew on
Until the curving line at last dissolved
Into that space where the perceiver
Becomes one with the object of perception
The hearer is reborn in what he hears,
The seer in the vision: Beethoven
Released from deafness into music,
Stravinsky from the prison of his dying.

## ROBERT GRAVES

## WHEN HE SAT WRITING
## (SONG FOR SHAKESPEARE'S BIRTHDAY, 1972)

When Will sat forging plays with busy friends
   He wrote no worse than they;
When he sat writing for his loves, and us,
   Such play outshone all play -
   And still it does today.

Comparisons are foolish: love alone
   Established Shakespeare's fame.
There's many a poet, laurelled on a throne,
   For whom the critics claim
   A like poetic flame.

Reject all rivals, even those richly blessed
   With histrionic art...
For groundlings he might jest, like all the rest,
   But suffered grief apart
   Mourning with his whole heart.

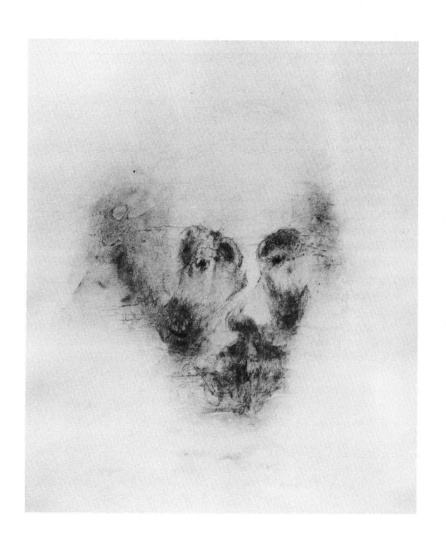

# TED HUGHES

## AN ALCHEMY

War in the egg
           Lustig the Moor
Aaron began it
           When Salt Tamora
In full blush of Lucretia
           Dawned on Leontes
Icicle Angelo
           Died Adonis' agony
Butchered by Richard
           The lineal Boar
Who darkened darkness
           With ravishing strides
And an Ass's horn
           To gore Titania
Queen of Fays
           For a pound of blood
Stinging Prince Hal
           To Portia's answer
Who defrocked
           Moses' Serpent
On the Hebrew Tree
           Anathalamia
Collapsed as Falstaff
           In the Boar's Head
The Knight of Venus
           After his Feast
Under Herne's acorns,
           Belated as bloated
A mushroom Caesar
           The wounds of Rome
Mouthing prophesy
           From which flittered
A mourning dove
Ancestral her sorcery
           Helena the Healer

Diana her owl side
                    Outwitted Angelo
Who walled up Ophelia
                            She wept to Othello
Willow Willow
                    As he lopped his rivals
A Fortinbras steeled
                            To close with Gertrude
Who came again

Desdemona rising
                    The Nun of Vienna
From killing her swine
                            The ring-dove's advent
Hamlet's muse
                        Hamlet's madness
Soused by Tempest
                        To Venus's Island
With her weird sisters
                            The blue Hag Hecate
Deflecting the dagger
                            With some rough magic
Into the Sanctum
                        Of Saintly Duncan
Double Macbeth
                        The crown's contagion
Drawn by the blade of Tarquin
                                Cordelia guiding
Blinded Gloucester
                        cutting to the brain
Then Lear saw nine-fold
                            The under-crown lightning
The Boar's Moons mangling
                            His sainted flesh

Lears Furens

He snapped its fang
                        It was Regan's body

31

He plucked out Goneril
                    Still it gored him
His third effort it vanished
                    And it had been his nothing
It had been his Joy
                    His truth beyond telling
In a warm body
                    Rock-dove of Aphrodite
Leaving a feather only

That Timon damned with gold

That carried Coriolanus
                    Crushed from Caesar
It was Old Nile's Serpent
                    Moon-browed Isis
Bride and Mother
                    Mourning a Rome
Leontes banished
                    Lear redivivus
Phoenix-Posthumous
                    Found breath in Marina
Redeemed all Tempest
                    His kiss of life
Stirred the Turtle
                    Of the waters of amnios
The lunar cauldron

The black Venus
                    double tongued
Swine-uddered Sycorax
                    Lilith the night-crow
Slid from the Tree

Released the Rainbow
                    Breasted Dove
With a leaf of light
                    Miranda with a miracle
To Adam Adonis

And sank
      In the crucible
            Tiamant
                 The Mother
The Scales
       The Coil
           Of the Matter
                  Deeper
Then ever plummet
            With Prospero's bones
And the sounding Book

## D.J. ENRIGHT

## ALL'S WELL THAT ENDS
## OR, SHAKESPEARE UNMASKED

I'm afraid he'll have to go.
He won't pass muster these days.

Black men he didn't like: he made them
Proud and gullible and jea. 34 ; and black
(Good fighters, but otherwise out of their depth).
He didn't like women, but neither
Was he a frank and manly homosexual.
'Woman delights not me: no, nor man neither...'
As for Jews, his complaint was that they were
Interested in money, were not Christians, and
If you pricked them they bled all over the place.
They deserved to have their daughters make
Unsuitable marriages.

(Put like that, Jews sound like a lot of us.
I shall have to rewrite this bit.)

A very dangerous man.
Think of all the trouble caused by that
Thoroughly offensive play of his, *Coriolanus*.
One night it wounded the feelings of the fascists,
The next it wounded the feelings of the communists.

He was anti-Scottish: it took an English army
To settle the hash of that kilted butcher
Macbeth.  He made jokes about the Welsh, the
French, the Danes, the Italians and the Spanish.
He accused a West Indian (or possibly Algerian)
Of trying to rape a white girl unsuccessfully.
If it wasn't a base Judean he displayed
As criminally careless with pearls, then
It was an equally base Indian. Thank God
He hadn't heard of the Australians!

To be sure, he was the servant of his public,
A rough unlettered lot, who rarely washed
And dwelt in the polluted alleys of London
Or the corners of slippery palaces. There wasn't
A drama critic of independent mind among them.
Even so, he must bear most of the blame,
He could have stayed in Stratford and led a
Quiet and useful life.

Worst of all, he believed in good and evil,
And mixed them up in a deliberately nasty
And confusing way. A shifty character,
He pictured the human conditions as one of
Unending and uneasy struggle, not to be
Resolved in a *haiku* or even a television
Debate. He made difficulties, he made
Much ado about nothing.

Now that we've stripped him clean
Of his poetry, we can see him plain.
Plainly he'll have to go.

## WOLE SOYINKA

## HAMLET

He stilled his doubts, they rose to halt and lame
A resolution on the rack. Passion's flame
Was doused in fear or error, his mind's unease
Bred indulgence to the state's disease.

Ghosts embowelled his earth; he clung to rails
In a gallery of abstractions, dissecting tales
As 'told by an idiot'. Passionless he set a stage
Of passion for the guilt he would engage.

Justice despaired. The turn and turn abouts
Of reason danced default to duty's couterpoint
Till treachery scratched the slate of primal clay
Then Metaphysics waived a thought's delay -
It took the salt in the wound, the 'point
Envenom'd too' to steel the prince of doubts.

**SEAMUS HEANEY**

**A FLOURISH FOR THE PRINCE OF DENMARK**

Ease him towards the strict arrest of bone,
this handler of beloved skulls. Let him
follow the worm of his thought
into the mound.

Set the ring-hoard's whorls like leeches
to his poison, borrow
the longship's swimming tongue
to carry his weight in words

for he must prove most royally.
Out of the silence a prow emerges
elaborate as a language
bursting its runes

outrunning shed alphabets
and oral harbourings:
a northerly migration, a southern breeze,
an English landfall.

## MICHAEL SCHMIDT

## THE FOOL

I warn you, said the fool,
I have a job to do.  I do it well.
I am the lowest rung on the man ladder:
my place, unchallenged, is not inconvenient

for I look up and undersee the polished boots
holed through utterly beneath, your hosiery
tattered at the knee, and you in silks outside
below are bare as apricots, as radishes.

Your bodies' downward scent is unperfumed.
I smell your misdemeanors and your motives.
-Yet every heart beats only from my heart
if it beats truly, though no voice speaks

my language,  None speaks truly.
In my rhetoric I am in the earth the undertaker,
the first worm who bears the licensed key
and unlocks every body: mine

is the first taste, my certificate
implies a corpse impure enough for plunder.
I am the deepest, oldest, thinnest fish
upon the seabed in the rocks and sand:

I see the world entire in looking up,
I intercept and touch the whale's long sound,
the prim sea-horse I watch grow old and faithless,
the sallow bladder-fish inflate and fawn

on sleek sea-kale trees that stand up like kings.
And yet I have no name but my two eyes,
my speech that none replies to,
a venerable antique uniform.

I have — I'm had on sufferance.
I am afraid of dark as much as you.
I pull my cap across my eyes and sleep.
I dream of an ignorant and sunny kingdom,

trivial, passionate, where all have hearts
within undisfigured bodies that are breathing
like men and women coming out of marble
into an actual day, as fish move out from weeds

blinding at the galleons that sink
and break before them on the seabed, spilling
treasure meaningless and brilliant, habitable;
and the drowned mariners more slowly drifting
touch down as gently dead as fallen leaves.

# ROY FULLER

## SHAKESPEARE AND CO

'Tis strange that death should sing - King John

Late Beethoven quartets: Stravinsky, old,
Murmuring 'Wonderful! Incredible!'
-Which leads the memoirist to name a third

'Who might have joined them', he who 'out of some
Terrible suffering' wrote *Macbeth* and *Lear*,
Then in his final years emerged to give

'Supreme expression' of the sense of life,
To wit *The Tempest* and *The Winter's Tale*.
One's touched, in the context, by his corny view,

Though sure that suffering's what we all can share
With genius and it needn't be top-notch.
The Victorian painter, Richard Dadd, who stabbed,

He said, 'an individual who called
Himself by father', made for forty years
In Broadmoor wonderful, incredible fairy worlds.

The difference is the hand's resource and craft
That urn the cloudy visions of the mind
Into a change of key, a pacifist isle.

Still, strange enough that autumn period:
The fruit so easily could be detached
But nature through its thread hangs on to add

Colour to seeds, a variegated cheek,
Flesh ready for consuming.  Chaos persists -
The troublesome reign, flase friends' conspiracies -

Though far from the ailments and obituaries
That almost daily plague old age, but yet
Can't spoil (that, rather, must enhance) the sense

Only possessed by age - that, when all's said
And done, life isn't death, however frail
The finger following the heavenly score.

# CHARLES CAUSLEY

## A WEDDING PORTRAIT

Look here, upon this picture, and on this.
*Hamlet,* Act III, Scene IV

Young man, young woman, gazing out
Straight-backed, straight-eyed, from what
    would seem
A cloud of sepia and cream,
In your twin pairs of eyes I note
A sense of the ridiculous,
Innocent courage, the strange hope
Things might get better in the lean
Year of the *Lusitania;* gas
Used at the Front; Arras and Ypres
More than place-names. Nineteen-fifteen.

My father, Driver Causley, stands
Speckless in 2nd Wessex kit,
A riding-crop in ordered hands,
Lanyard well-slicked, and buttons lit
With Brasso; military cap
On the fake pillar for an urn.
Khaki roughens his neck. I see
The mouth half-lifted by a scrap
Of smile. It is a shock to learn
How much, at last, he looks like me.

Serene, my mother wears a white
And Sunday look, and at her throat
The vague smudge of a brooch, a mute
Pale wound of coral. The smooth weight
Of hair curves from her brow; gold chain
Circles a wrist to mark the day,
And on the other is the grey
Twist of a bandage for the flame
That tongued her flesh as if to say,
'I am those days that are to come'.

As I walk by them on the stair
A small surprise of sun, a ruse
Of light, gives each a speaking air,
A sudden thrust, though both refuse
- Silent as fish or water-plants -
To break the narrow stream of glass
Dividing us. I was nowhere
That wedding-day, and the pure glance
They shaft me with acknowledges
Nothing of me. I am not here.

The unregarding look appears
To say, somehow, man is a breath,
And at the end hides in the fire,
In bolting water, or the earth.
I am a child again, and move
Sunwards these images of clay,
Listening for their first birth-cry.
And with the breath my parents gave
I warm the cold words with my day:
Will the dead-weight to fly. To fly.

## PETER PORTER

## EXIT, PURSUED BY A BEAR

*Others abide our question. Thou art free.*
Art not an artist but an industry,
And to a nation fallen on hard times
Worth more than North Sea Oil or Yorkshire Mines:
Indeed, our Bardric tours and Shakespeare tomes,
With the Royal Family, Scotch and Sherlock Holmes,
Convince the U.S.A. and E.E.C.
That though we're not what once we used to be
If there's some sale which needs a bit of class
An English accent's all that you can ask -
Our actors, raised on Bolingbroke and York,
Can hold their own at late-night TV Talk,
Directors trained by England's classic teachers
Bring something more to Ads and Second Features,
And poet-dons, with ear and taste defective,
On Sixteenth Century love-life turn detective,
Track amorous ladies with Italian looks
Through sonnets, diaries, letters and part books.
Our GNP, from Inverness to Flatford,
Could take a hint from tourist-battered Stratford:
An asset nursed need never be depleted,
The English Language cannot be defeated.

We owe this to the man for whom we're here,
Our Superstar, our J.C., our Shakespeare,
And if one's heart sinks in the London Library
Or trying to work the BM without bribery
Confronted with the Shakespeare section looming
Above us like a ship's hull (that's assuming
This metaphor impresses jet-age readers)
The mind, the most debased of dirty feeders,
Is more than pleased to see four hundred years
Of parasitic comment raised in tiers,
Unsought, unread, uncared-for and undusted,
The whole life's work for which dead men once lusted,
Grabbed office, wheedled, schemed and struggled
    through,
Reduced to Nothing after Much Ado.

44

But exegesis lives and dies, it's not
(whatever you may think, you Clan of Kott)
The point: we've got the plays in fine editions,
We know interpolations and omissions,
And may, setting scholarship among the sins then,
Say Shakespeare wrote *The Two Noble Kinsmen* -
At least the very best bits - and then stretch a
Point and reassign to worthy Fletcher
All that tedious play, *King Henry the Eighth,*
Like Wolsey's bladders, not much puffed of late.
Whilst praising Shakespeare, let us not forget
Contemporaries who left us in their debt,
Those men whom Swinburne praised in Mermaid dress:
The more of Middleton's is not the less
Of Shakespeare's glory and *The Broken Heart,*
If not quite *Antony,* is stunning art -
May they receive as many new productions
As teenage Romeos their set seductions
(See Martin Amis's *The Rachel Papers*
For the latest slant on young love cutting capers) -
Let all the kudos this great name has stored
Be used to recommend the plays of Ford.


But now, alas, I reach the nasty part
Of this encomium - dramatic art
Is only half alive upon the page:
What then of Shakespeare on the modern stage?
I've sat through *Troilus* in the Second Empire,
Lear in Local Government, 'one that gathers samphire,
Dreadful trade!' but surely not of Dover's
Since Edgar's dressed to play for Bristol Rovers,
*Macbeth* in trench coats and his guilt Lady
Somnambulising fully-frontal, Brady
And Hindley to the life, as if the Bard
Were playing understudy to de Sade -

Then *Hamlet* "en risotto", lines all diced
And dished up like a bowl of savoury rice -
Still, none of this is quite as bad as what
TV has done - sans time, sans lines, sans plot,
Sans everything but window dressing, got
Through with much relief! Since money's time,
The classics on the Box can be a crime.
Then there's Shakespeare politicised by Brecht,
Hung-up by Brook, portrayed by Bond and wrecked
In any one of twenty thousand ways -
The mortal genius of some thirty plays,
Whose "lives", as Mr. Schoenbaum rightly says,
Are many as a cat's, since each enhancer
Sees him like himself, a necromancer,
A Catholic, a crypto-queer, a Cornish Warlock
(He only lacks his own "Person from Porlock"),
But always there behind that Stratford bust
Or in those undug feet of common dust
The Grand Enigma of all generations,
Surviving even fashion and translation,
And like his favourite Ovid ever changing
Gods and men in Nature, re-arranging
The world we others fancy is opaque,
Or cannot understand or simply fake,
Until it seems Creation's paradigm,
A timeless dream which yet unfolds in time.

I'll finish now this commonplace recital
By just explaining why I chose its title -
It's from, of course you know, *The Winter's Tale;*
The man the bear rended tooth and nail
Was loyal Antigonus, the child Perdita,
One of the nicest heroines by far,
Too good to serve up as an ursine entree -
But think, the man who put her in the play
Had daughters of his own, and how did he
Treat them, his wife, his son, his family?

One fact alone I dare to say tonight:
*Shakespeare's younger daughter couldn't write,*
Her mark is on some document, a cross -
Imagination must be at a loss
To think his mind, though blackened by its spouse's,
Cared less for daughters than for Stratford houses!
It opens up the way for royal Lear,
An avenue of anger lit by fear -
The bear is death which chases him so long
And never can be  quietened by a song,
The creatures of the plays are funeral mutes
Lamenting Orpheus and his broken lute,
And on some dismal shore the bones are cracked,
The genius of the universe ransacked.

## GEORGE MACBETH

## THE CRETINS

O heavens! is't possible a young maid's wits
Should be as mortal as an old man's life?
*Hamlet,* Act IV, Scene V

I

There was something about that night,
        and the restaurant, and the food:
we thought about Proust, and his book,
        and both remembered the past

as we ate our bread and cheese,
        and watched the flow of the sea
where it seemed to move like a river
        away towards the West.

I thought about Normandy,
        and the beaches that other June
nearly thirty years before
        and the storm the night they came.

And then it happened: the moment
        changed, and defined for ever
by a tiny incident
        so rich it burned like a sore.

II

They were brought along the shore
    led by a group of nuns,
all dressed in their plain blue scarves:
    and they stopped for the setting sun.

They stood with their arms held wide,
    and their heavy faces fixed
on the simple glow in the air:
    and some of them sang a hymn.

It was piteous, it was grim.
    I felt the long tears wax
in my eyes as the red ball fell
    into the sea, and died.

From the window, I could see
    the pleasure it gave their minds
blocked from the cradle, to feel
    the last heat of the day

and to take its joy on their skin
    and to hold it gently there,
more full of its dwindling fire
    than anyone else could be

## PATRICIA BEER

## SEVEN AGES

Where have I got to in the seven-act play?
Where was I ever? No doubt as a baby
I bawled and vomited as the script says.
I wasn't acting and I don't remember.
I wriggle in the anecdotes of aunts.
And when I get to second childishness
And mere oblivion I shan't be conscious
Or hear the anecdotes of my decay.

Three of the parts I never really played:
I couldn't cycle fast enough to school,
I fell in love but never wrote about it,
The career I took up called for little action.
The fifth is more like me; I must be there.
The justice is well-fed, well-heeled, censorious,
Torn between general and particular,
Dodging at dawn the chill of two-sevenths left.

Shakespeare knew the importance of 'as if'.
He knew it was the only way to act
And that to live as if there were a hell
Is very like living as if there weren't.
Anything better than the anxiety dream
Of being on the stage without a part,
Especially in a long play: seven acts
Although the first and last are played in darkness.

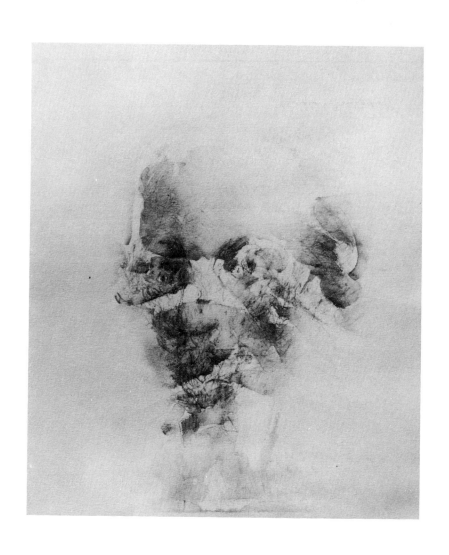

## ANTHONY THWAITE

## A GIRDLE ROUND THE EARTH

'King Rear was foorish man his girls make crazy'
Says something certainly about the play.
'Prutus fall on sord for bolitical reason'
Its unambiguous, though not the way
We native-speakers might have put it, who share
A language with the undoubted global poet.
In Tokyo or Benghazi, he abides
Our questioning syllabus still, will never stay
For an answer as the candidates all stare
Into the glossaried cryptograms he hides.

O Saku Seppiya, Shakhs Bey-er, O you
Who plague the schools and universities
From Patagonia to Pakistan,
From Thailand to Taiwan, how would it please
Your universal spirit to look down
And see the turbans and burnouses bent
Above your annotated texts, or see
*Simplified Tales from Lamb* by slow degrees
Asphyxiate the yellow and the brown?
To pick up the quotation, 'thou art free'-


But Matthew Arnold, schools inspector, who
Saw you 'self-school'd, self-scann'd', could not have known
How distantly from Stratford and the Globe
With British Council lecturers you've flown:
Midsummer Nights in Prague and Kathmandu,
Polonius stabbed dressed in a gallabiyah,
Shylock the Palestinian refugee,
And Hamlet's father's Serbo-Croat groan,
Dunsinane transported to Peru,
Kabuki for All's Well, Noh for King Lear.

'To be or not to be.  Is that a question?'
The misquotations littering the page,
The prose translations fingermarked with sweat,
You prove again, world-wide, 'not of an age
But for all time', the English Ala' ad-Din,
The Western Chikamatsu, more than both
And different from either, somehow worth
Those sun-baked hours in echoing lecture-halls,
On torn tatami or dune-drifted stage:
'Lady Macbeth is houswif full of sin'
'Prince Hel is drinkard tho of nobel berth'.

# JOHN HEATH-STUBBS

## WINTER IN ILLYRIA

The fountain is choked, yellow leaves
Drift on the broken pavement.
( *'And the rain it raineth'.* )

A white peacock
Screams from a windraked arbour.
( *'Come away, Death.'* )

Remembered echoes - echoes of lute-strings,
Echoes of drunken singing.
( *'By swaggering could I never thrive.'* )

Cries of a tormented man, shamed
In a darkened room.
( *'Carry his water to the wise woman!'* )

He left feckless Illyria, changed
His name, enlisted in the army
( *'I'll be revenged on the whole pack of you.'* )

In the neighbouring state of Venice, rose to the
    rank of Ancient
Personal assistant to the General.
( *'Put money in thy purse.'* )

## BRIAN PATTEN

## THE MAIN CHARACTER

The hero thinks the hero is the main character,
The heroine thinks the heroine is the main character,
The audience is enthralled but has
Not much say in the matter.
For the main character is still out in the wings,
He has not yet appeared.
Appalling crimes are committed.
Appalling sorrows crawl across the stage and fall
Into the laps of the audience.
Ambitions are proven absurd,
Times are slaughtered,
Great speeches are made and revoked,
The stage is set for a major revelation but still
The main character sits in the wings
Twiddling his thumbs.
For no one has told him exactly what it is he must do
To bring the play to a fruitful conclusion,
And so the play goes on and on
And appalling crimes are committed,
And great speeches are made and revoked
And still the main character sits exhausted in the wings
Twiddling his thumbs.

# JAMES MERRILL

## THE SCHOOL PLAY

'Harry of Hereford, Lancaster, and Derby,
Stands here for God, his country, and ...'And what?
'Stands here for God, his Sovereign, and himself,'
Growled Captain Fry who had the play by heart.
I was the First Herald, 'a small part'
— I was small too - 'but an important one.'
What was not important to the self
At nine or ten? Already I had crushes
On Mowbray, Bushy, and the Duke of York.
Handsome Donald Niemann (now himself,
According to the Bulletin, headmaster
Of his own school somewhere out West) awoke
Too many self-indulgent mouthings in
The dummy mirror before smashing it,
For me to set my scuffed school cap at him.
Another year I'd play that part myself,
Or Puck, or Goneril, or Prospero.
Later, in adolescence, it was thought
Clever to speak of having found oneself,
With a smile and rueful headshake for those who hadn't.
People still do. Only the other day
A woman my age told us that her son
"Hadn't found himself" — at thirty-one!
I heard in mind's ear an amused hum
Of mothers and fathers from behind the curtain,
And that flushed, far-reaching hour came back
Months of rehearsal in the gymnasium
Had led to: when the skinny nobodies
Who'd memorized the verse and learned to speak it
Emerged in beards and hose (or gowns and rouge)
Vivid with character, having put themselves
All unsuspecting into the masters' hands.

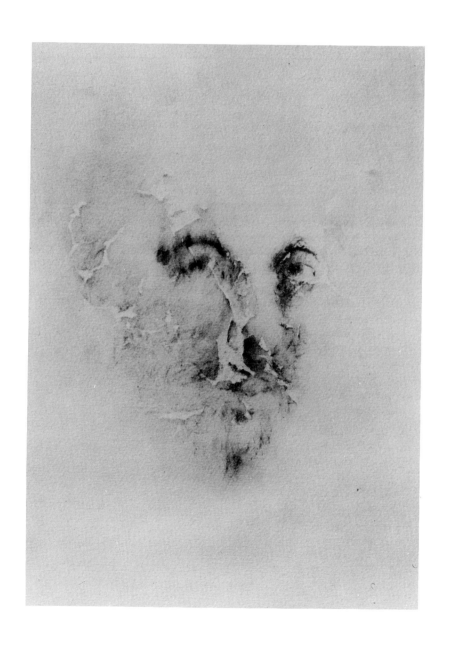

## EDWIN MORGAN

## INSTRUCTIONS TO AN ACTOR

Now, boy, remember this is the great scene.
You'll stand on a pedestal behind a curtain,
the curtain will be drawn, and then you don't move
for eighty lines; don't move, don't speak, don't breathe.
I'll stun them all out there, I'll scare them,
make them weep, but it depends on you.
I warn you eighty lines is a long time,
but you don't breathe, you're dead,
you're a dead queen, a statue,
you're dead as stone, new-carved,
new-painted and the paint not dry
—we'll get some red to keep your lip shining—
and you're a mature woman, you've got dignity,
some beauty still in middle age, and
you're kind and true, but you're dead,
your husband thinks you're dead,
the audience thinks you're dead,
and you don't breathe, boy, I say
you don't even blink for eighty lines,
if you blink you're out!
Fix your eye on something and keep watching it.
Practise when you get home. It can be done.
And your move at last — music's the cue.
When you hear a mysterious solemn jangle
of instruments, make yourself ready.
Five lines more, you can lift a hand.
It may tingle a bit, but lift it—
slow, slow—
O this is where I hit them
right between the eyes, I've got them now—
I'm making the dead walk—
you move a foot, slow, steady, down
you guard your balance in case you're stiff,
you move, you step down, down from the pedestal,
control your skirt with one hand, the other hand
you now hold out—

O this will melt their hearts if nothing does—
to your husband who wronged you long ago
and hesitates in amazement
to believe you are alive.
Finally he embraces you, and there's nothing
I can give you to say, boy,
but you must show that you have forgiven him.
Forgiveness, that's the thing. It's like a second life.
I know you can do it. —Right then, shall we try?

# ELAINE FEINSTEIN

## 'WE WILL YET DO WELL.'
*Antony and Cleopatra, III.xi.*

Forgotten, shabby and long time abandoned
   in stubbled fur, with broken
teeth like toggles, the old gods are leaving
   They will no longer crack the
tarmac of the language, open generous
   rivers, heal our scoured thoughts.
They will only blink, and move on, and
   tomorrow no-one will remember their songs

unless they rise in warning, as when
   sudden planes speed overhead
crossing the sky with harsh accelerating
   screams pitched high. You may shiver
then to hear the music of the gods leaving,
   the quiet words of hope sadden me more.
Who was ever noble without a
   reckless heart? This generation
is waiting for the boy Octavius.
   They don't like losers.
And the gods are leaving us.

## GEORGE BARKER

## CRITICAL SONNET FOR WILLIAM SHAKESPEARE

*Anon as patient as the female dove*
*When that her golden couplets are disclosed*
*His silence will sit drooping.*
                  *Hamlet,* V.i.

What most I wish to hear from you I heard.
It was the silence in between the speaking,
the golden silences that charged the word
with correspondences I had been seeking
in all vocables.  But only your
silences like the patient female dove
disclosed the secret I had been looking for:
language is the golden cage of our love.

It is as though the heart, adoring silence
but tortured by the ghouls of its existence,
cried out howling in the night, or sang
wildly of love in dreams of violence,
or till its suffering, cracked at the final pang,
out of the dead mouths of children rang.

# JOHN WAIN

## JULIET AND HER NURSE

Under the hot slanting Italian sun,
two woman-shapes.

This one casting a lean upright shadow:
that one casting a soft rounded shadow.

Here, all quickness, insistence:
there, a habit of circling.

And why should she not circle?
She ranges for nourishment far distant.

Her landscape lies spread beneath the crags
where she sits memoried, brooding: she sails out
on broad dusty wings now and then,
to look it over.

And why should she not be insistent?
She, she: haec, illa: our tongue does not say it.
Needs newly awakened are needles.
One night in his arms is a down payment:
the rest is to come soon, it must come, it must.

They are like water:
this one leaping from the rock, unwarmed, unstained,
exclaiming in diamond spray, avid for contact,
contact with stone, wood, clay, air, skin,
with the throats of animals and men:
that one broadened out, standing,
in places very deep, calm on the surface,
in places shaded by old trees.

The young woman is hungry.
She wants love, which is to say that she wants suffering,
joy, fury, repletion and forgiveness.
She wants to throw herself over the steep rocks.

The old woman is satisfied:
her body moves slowly and needs little,
stored with rich protein of her memories.

Memories of the rose-crystal dawn when she, too,
cast a lean upright shadow:
when she threw herself over the steep rocks
and he was standing below, eager, and caught her.

The young woman will not be caught.
Down the rock-face dashes the clear water
unwarmed, unstained: wasted:
no old trees will shade her,
there will be no quiet depths.
We know the story.

## ELIZABETH JENNINGS

## FOR SHAKESPEARE: A POET'S TRIBUTE

We forget you are there
Not out of negligence but because you live
in our blood and nerves, in every brain cell too.
To us who attempt to sing and state you give
A bonus of presents at birth and this you do
    Before we notice. We hear

As children a travesty of
Your words, are led unwittingly into your mind.
Then at school, sometimes reluctantly, we see
The shining words before our eyes, we find
Your presence around us as you set us free
    With the gentleness of love

To pursue the cruel and sweet
Vocation of making worlds. You are a debt
Leaping from every lasting line we write,
And yet with what ingratitude we forget
That you are pouring upon us your radiant light.
    And when we know defeat

You teach us the patience to
Wait with respect upon language, learn our trade
Over and over. When we are silent you
Echo to us from the sounds of the worlds you've made.
You bell us back with pride to what we can do.
    All this owe to you.

## MIROSLAV HOLUB

## POLONIUS

Behind every arras
he does his duty
unswervingly.
Walls are his ears,
keyholes his eyes.

He slinks up the stairs,
oozes from the ceiling,
floats through the door
ready to give evidence,
prove what is proven,
stab with a needle
or pin on an order.

His poems always rhyme,
his brush is dipped in honey,
his music flutes
from marzipan and cane.

You buy him
by weight, boneless,
a pound of wax flesh,
a pound of mousey philosophy,
a pound of jellied
flunkey.

And when he's sold out
and the left-overs wrapped
in a tasselled obituary,
a paranoid funeral notice,

and when the spore-creating mould
of memory
covers him over,
when he falls
arse-first to the stars,

the whole continent will be lighter,
earth's axis straighten up
and in night's thunderous arena
a bird will chirp in gratitude.

*Translated from the Czech by*
*Ian Milner and George Theiner*

**RAFAEL ALBERTI**

**ROMEO AND JULIET**

How still your body now, wordless
and pure in shape, blue; motionless
and oval tears entomb your dreams.

Ornate keys with ogre-handles
harmonising your flesh and blood
without dividing head from thighs.

Always standing in one spot, my eyes
that by their sober gleam keep watch
make me want to travel with your body.

O youthful sea, O naked ocean
with only fifteen pallid moons, leading
to the sky and unmapped countries!

*Translated from the Spanish by*
*Alan Sillitoe*

**PETER HUCHEL**

**OPHELIA**

Later, in the morning,
Towards the white dawn,
Boots wading
In the shallow water,
Poles poking,
A raucous command;
They raise the muddy
Bow-net of barbed wire.

No Kingdom,
Ophelia,
Where a scream
Hollows the water
And a magic spell
Shatters
The bullet
On a willow leaf.

*Translated from the German by*
*Henry Beissel*

## PENELOPE SHUTTLE

## THE PRETTY WORM

'Hast thou the pretty worm of Nilus there...'

One summer I dreamt
I Kept a snake for my pet

He moved with the ease of fire
He was a soul of fertility,
more pliant than the birds
as they turn and wheel in the air

I loved the cool clarity of the asp

Coiled, he slept
as if at the floodmark of the uterus

I fed him on saucers of milk,
my immortal, my baby

One day, being clumsey, I spilt the milk,
and he hissed, silver rage

I froze
and all my memories trembled
How to escape his fatel kiss,
the foetal grace of his venom?

His antigue tongue stroked the air

'the snake who knows no charm'

I grasped him by his throat
He turned to rope and bound me fast,
my nipple the knot,
my breath relapsing into draperies,
rich obscured histories

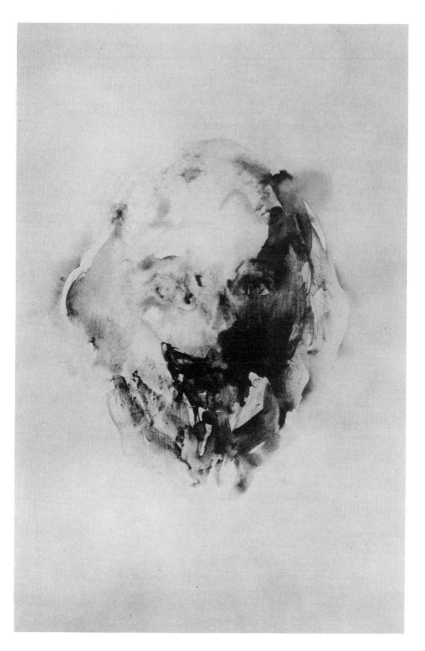

## CRAIG RAINE

## IN MODERN DRESS

A pair of blackbirds
warring in the roses,
one or two poppies

losing heir heads,
the rampled lawn
a battlefield of dolls.

Branch by pruned branch,
a child has climbed
the family tree

to queen it over us:
we groundlings search
the flowering cherry

till we find her face,
its pale prerogative
to rule our hearts.

Sir Walter Raleigh
trails his comforter
about the muddy garden,

a full-length Hilliard
in miniature hose
and padded pants.

How rakishly upturned
his fine moustache
of oxtail soup,

foreshadowing, perhaps,
some future time
of altered favour,

if not the high chair
like a pillory, features
pelted with food.

So many expeditions
to learn the history
of this little world:

I watch him grub
in the vegetable patch
and ponder the potato

in its natural state
for the very first time,
or found a settlement

of leaves and sticks
cleverly protected
by a circle of stones.

But where on earth
did he manage to find
that cigarette end?

Rain and wind.
The day disintegrates.
I observe the lengthy

inquisition of a worm
then go indoors to face
a scattered armada

of picture hooks
on the dining room floor,
the remains of a ruff

on my glass of beer,
Sylvia Plath's *Ariel*
drowned in the bath.

Washing hair, I kneel
to supervise a second rinse
and act the courtier:

tiny seed pearls,
tingling into sight,
confer a kind of majesty.

And I am author
of this toga'd tribune
on my aproned lap,

who plays his part
to an audience of two,
repeating my words.

## DAVID SWEETMAN

## SHAKESPEARE COUNTRY

Confetti at the lych-gate or distance gulls
wheeling over a tip...?
Even so, she smiles, secretly pregnant
and thinks of tomorrow through the memory
of grass flatterned as the baize
where a General finger-taps
imitating farmers yanking boots from the mud,
astronauts upon a new gravity.

With a flourish their muckspreader
signs a declaration of war
and the General retires to his bunker.
Draymen place depth-charges
beneath a village pub where the barmaid
records a successful strike
for a stockbroker who's telling her
how he hates taxes and blacks.

The lawn is shell-shocked: a plump insect
(gangly as a watch tower)
is ignored by the foam frog
(making love atop an explosion)
while way below, the old General
launches our last wave and night encloses
the Christmas turkey, its insides
outside, bloodied from its beak.

## DANNIE ABSE

## IN THE OLD AGE HOME WHERE HE SAYS HE'S RESTING

he tree-watches, this autumn, zany Prospero,
ex-stage magician, old star of the lost Empires,
at the window, his powered face perfect gallows.

Look our own eidolon! Between daft paragraphs
he hums 'Daisy, Daisy' chuckles mildewed jokes
and waits for condescending visitors to laugh.

Like that tree, his mind's half ruined. Again
   complains
but not of Caliban: 'Son, any child could tell
this place needs renovating, cant't you smell the
drains?

Or grumbles:'Any child could tell they steal my
   clothes;'
suspects the Superintendent's snazzy shirt is his
before switching off to a mouth-gaping doze,

to the bleak mechanism. How molesting it
always is, the last real act. Does Miranda neglect him
now he cannot summon music from the Pit?

Prospero snores on. Ariel is unconfined, free,
and any child could tell but none will tell the child,
'Tis magic, magic, that hath ravished thee.'

## DAVID WRIGHT

### REMEMBERING AVON
*Near Stratford,* 1940

He is, of course, the genius of the place.
That is, of midland England, whose flatness
Rescues it from unreasonable beauty;
A pleasant, unremarkable country
Watered by its river Avon, whose source is
The middle point of England, near Naseby.

I knew its reaches well: at least from Evesham
As far as Warwick. Then I was a boy
And it was the summer armadas came over
With the full moon, flying to Birmingham
And back again, unladen, in the morning.
I saw the cattle drowsing in the fields,
And black elms ponder over scarcely pacing
Water, while white spokes of light, far off,
Walked on the Horizon until All Clear.
And there my boat lay, floating on the water,
Well above Bidford; ready to go on.

The time, like all times, furious; my voyage
Frivolous, without aim, peripheral.
But now I feel its meaning, as I did then,
A realization that a golden age
Exists; at all times, though no age is golden;
And that it is enough to see it once:
A derelict park, receding pastoral,
And intense present, ever caught between
All that must be because of what has been.

# CHARLES TOMLINSON

## VARIATION

*And there is nothing left remarkable*
*Beneath the visiting moon.*

*Antony and Cleopatra, IV.vii.*

What is left remarkable beneath the visiting moon
    Is the way the horizon discovers itself to be
The frontier of a country unseen till this:
    Soon the light will focus the whole of it
Under one steadying beam, but now in rising
    Still has to clear the brow of a hill
To unroll the unmapped differences here,
    Where the floor of the valley refuses to appear
Uncoped by the shadow of its flank: it is the speed
    That accompanies this deed of climbing and revealing
Marks the acent: you can measure out the pace
    Of the unpausing visitant between tree and tree,
Setting each trunk alight, then hurrying on
    To shine back down over the entire wood
It has ignited to flicker in white.  Free
    From the obstructions it has come burning through
It has the whole of the night sky to review
    The world below it, seeming to slow
And even to dream its way.  It does not arrive alone
    But carries the memory of that spread of space
And of the aeons across which it has shone till now
    From the beginning. This is the illumination it pours
Into the shadows and the watcher's mind,
    As it touches on planes of roofs it could not foresee
Shaping and sharing its light when it set out
    In a rain of disintegrating comets, of space creating.

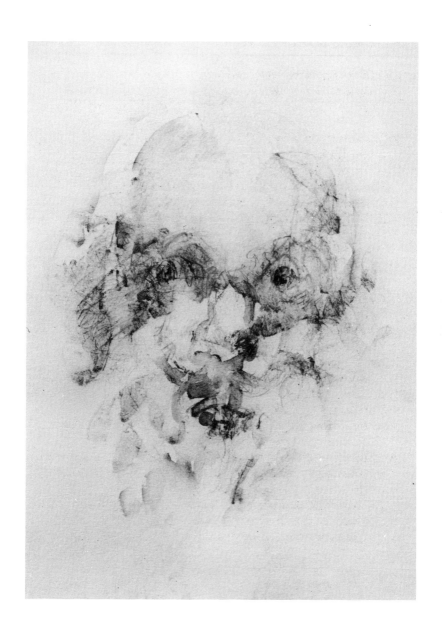

# DAVID HARSENT

## THE ANALYSAND

*I have had a dream, past the wit of man to say*
*what dream it was.* A Midsummer Night's Dream

Just on the cusp of sleep
the image of a hare, hunkered
in the lee of a blackthorn hedge,

a sloping snowfield, a spinney,
the moon like a crooked sixpence...
She'd expected to know the place.

It was dawn from the smell
of bacon in the pan
and the brisk riddling of coals.

She fetched him out, his boots
breaking the snowcrust
in Church Lane, the dogs at heel;

and, oh, he did it perfectly—
clapping against the cold
so that the sound

could reach her at one remove;
stopping to watch a heron;
lifting one hand, like someone

bowling under-arm,
to release the dogs.  A rustle
of breath like silver-leaf

touched his lips as he started
to tackle the hill.
In that air, she could see

prisms in the spindrift
off his toecaps. No matter;
she was smug with speed.

As he stamped up
the steepest pitch, just past
the spinney and rose

towards her (so close
that she almost laughed)
she leapt into wakefulness.

*   *   *

I can't tell why,
but the most important part
was fetching him out:

his handclap coming at me
a pulse-beat late, the way
he set the dogs running.

I was lying-up
in the lee of a hedge; even so,
I could see everything

as if I sat on his shoulder;
and it came, remember,
on the cusp of sleep.

Didn't you say
those are the truest dreams?
Well, I was puss,

a flibbertigibbet, familiar
to some wise old woman.
What do you make of it? Is he still

working the dogs on the down?
Will my children be harelipped
and my gaze mildew the grain?

# List of Poets Represented

Ted Hughes.

C. Day Lewis.

W.H. Auden.

Stephen Spender.

Robert Graves.

D.J. Enright.

Wole Soyinka.

Seamus Heaney.

Michael Schmidt.

Roy Fuller.

Peter Porter.

George Macbeth.

Patricia Beer.

Anthony Thwaite.

John Heath-Stubbs.

Brian Patten.

James Merrill.

Edwin Morgan.

Elaine Feinstein.

George Barker.

John Wain.

Elizabeth Jennings.

Rafael Alberti.

Miroslav Holub.

Peter Huchel.

Penelope Shuttle.

Craig Raine.

David Sweetman.

Dannie Abse.

David Wright.

David Harsent.